Sucking Mud

By

Barbara Eustice Cooper

Sucking Mud

Barbara Eustice Cooper

Publisher: Cross Wise Publishing
http://crosswisepublishing.com

ISBN-13:978-0615968247
ISBN-10:0615968244

Dedication

To The Precious Holy Spirit!
He gave me the name of the book, and all of the chapter titles. He was with me guiding me all the way. Thank you!

BARBARA EUSTICE COOPER grew up primarily in Shreveport, Louisiana. Her experience with Alcohol Addiction affords her a unique and personal insight into the vicious cycle that is all too common with addictions, whether or not alcohol based.

Her walk through life as an alcoholic began at age 17, and ended at age 36. Barbara bares her soul as she graphically describes how alcohol made her vulnerable to boorish men, as well as the countless other cruelties that alcoholism notoriously inflicts upon its victims.

The best part of this writing is where Barbara chronicles the day and hour at which she made a decision that would change her life permanently, and for the better.

She believes the same grace that empowered her to overcome her addictions is available to everyone; thus the motivation behind the writing of this book. She has a strong desire to reach out to those who may feel just as helpless and hopeless, as she once did.

Although her book painfully recounts the many hardships that alcohol addictions bring into a person's life, she willingly shares her heartfelt testament of how never giving up, on herself or God, has brought her to 37 years of sobriety.

The walk through this book was very painful for the author; nonetheless, it was done sacrificially for the sake of others who need to know there is a permanent way out.

She knows she heard the Audible voice of God, and wishes to share His truths with you, the reader.

Unfortunately, I thought Booze was my friend

Greetings reader,

I truly believe you've found this book by divine intervention, so I wanted to welcome you and tell you a little about the book before you read it.

This is a true story that begins with me in the hospital where I find myself feeling lost and forced to look at the reason I have reached such depths of despair. Maybe you have been drawn to this book because you, or someone you know may be feeling that same sense of despair as well.

My circumstances forced me into a state of introspection, facing up to the truth, and taking the blame for where I was.

It was at that point I came to realize I could no longer blame other people in my life for my mistakes. I realized that I needed to take a step back, and make an effort to understand and forgive the humanity of others as a starting point to understand myself.

Yes, when bad things happen in a young child's life it can affect how that person reacts to their world. However, if I learned nothing else I learned that it is foolish to allow negative experiences to drive life choices.

I fell into a pit where my choice of excesses soon became my primary reason for living. Once God showed me that I could not continue to use my childhood experiences as an excuse to choose excesses, and blame others for those choices, my life took a drastic turn for the better.

I realized there had came a time that I had to look into the mirror for more than just to see if my makeup was on straight!

Walk with me through this painful time and see how God brought me to victory at the end!
Barbara

Table of Contents

As I wake up to the smell of a hospital wondering how I got there, there is a little tickle in my mind of what I had been doing. I had been on a three day binge of drinking with little food, taking the children to Joanne's for her to watch. The plan was to drive off the overpass that would kill me.

As I was driving I would take a drink of the peppermint snaps that I had between my legs. I saw a young man hitchhiking and picked him up, we didn't go very far before he was begging me to let him out of the car.

I arrive at Joanne's mobile home, taking off my wedding ring, as a declaration of my marriage at an end I felt that what I was going to do would bring me the peace that I so desperately longed for. I drove off and was stopped by a Lady and her Son (they were Jewish, later on that pleased me greatly)

The young Man drove my car and took me to the doctor and there to my surprise was Joanne. She had already made arrangements for the doctor to admit to the hospital.
Joanne revealed to me that as soon as I left she was praying for someone to stop me, and at that time she put my wedding ring in my purse.

On the way to the hospital I told her to drive me through Taco Bell, where I bought way more than I could eat in fact way more than three people could eat, but when I was coming off a drunk I always bought too much food and the room reeked of Mexican food. They tried to make me go to the Psychiatric floor.

A Doctor and Nurse entered the room. I replied my husband! He said "Vell vhat is wrong with him? "I said he is breathing ! "Vell, if he vasn't breathing he vould be dead ??" I said you got it doc !! At that they left the room I wondered how long did he go to school? He couldn't tell the difference between a crazy person and a drunk??

I didn't want to see my husband so I asked the Nursing staff to put No Visitors on my door in the hopes it would keep him from seeing me. No such luck in he came mad as an old wet hen, I had no business being in the hospital!

He demanded that I check out of the hospital No! I refused, he was mad as I said but he was always mad when he didn't get his way. The only good thing about his raising such a fuss with me I was still drunk and it didn't bother me as it would usually. He was always unhappy unless he got his way.

As I was trying to figure out my options I realized I had burned all of my bridges. I just couldn't go back to Louisiana with another failed marriage or relationship. I had put my family through so very much already. So the question was where to go, how do I get away from my husband. I didn't realize at the time it was more than escaping Cooper, it was my life that I had messed up.

Lying there I sought sleep and found it, but there had to be a reckoning about my choices, how had I gotten where I was, not physically but where was my head? The thought of going back was so scary, not pleasant by any means. Somehow I found the courage to open up all the horrible things I had done. It seemed like a bad movie, going back to age fifteen.

Little Girl Lost

As the memories of the past came to my mind I see a troubled child unsure of how to behave. All of my life I realized I didn't fit in, not the way regular people did. I was a child with attention deficit disorder, in those days a child was labeled a trouble maker I didn't fit in anywhere.

My home life as a child was good as long as I was able to live with my Mama (my Mother's Mother). She was a wonderful Godly woman, that when I got up in the morning she was sitting at the table with her Bible and her coffee. She loved the Lord with all her heart and even to a child it was obvious that she was real.

Because of my last name I was teased all the time, today it would be called bulling .Not only was I ADD I was also dyslexic. Because of these things it made learning very hard. I would study but couldn't seem to retain anything. I had no help at all with my homework, so very often I didn't finish the work. I got called down a lot about that. I was not allowed to have any friends over to my house, I wasn't allowed to go to other people's sleep over's. I was a very lonely child. I was as lost as it I had been taken far away. This would be a painful part of my life that lasted always.

Family

The home we lived in when my Mother married Harold was an angry house. He had a volatile temper; the smallest thing would set him off. We could be eating a meal and something would trigger his temper. Besides the cussing he was liable to knock off all of the bowls of food on the floor. The air in our house was loaded with fear of what would happen next.

He kept a loaded gun beside the bed. I would wake up needing to go to the bathroom but I was afraid that he would shoot me. Finally I would stand at my bedroom door and say daddy I have to go to the bathroom.

I had few friends for my Mother didn't want children to come to our house or me to go to theirs. The Christmas I was nine I got a bicycle with a basket on it. It gave me the freedom that I desired. Mother would let me ride for thirty to forty-five minutes then I would have to check in with her.

I knew everyone in out neighborhood, when I saw older people out I would stop and talk with them. It also opened a new life for me for she would let me go to the library. I would call her at work and say I was going, and then when I got home I would call her to say I was home safe. I was able to check out five books at a time and would have them read in a day and a half.

In the books I left my home and troubles and became whomever I was reading about. Before the summer was over I had read everything that appealed to me, with my Mother's permission I was able to read books from, the adult section. My first find was Earle Stanley Gardner, Perry Mason. I inhaled those books. It became the love of mine to see the bad people get caught!

Harold was rarely mad at me, took me places with him on the weekends. He was an electrician and these were jobs he did on the side. He would have me crawl under houses and to pull wires through. Thinking back I am so glad that there were no snakes under the house. As the memories of the past come to my mind I see a trouble child unsure of how to behave.

.I was so blessed to have my Mama who was Noveline's Mother. She was so different than my mother; in fact she didn't have anything in common with anyone that was kin to us. Noveline and my Daddy met as he was in an army convey passing through Minden. Because of a jeep wreck he was brought to Minden Hospital where he met my Mother. Convoys were a familiar site as it was October 1941. Germany was at war with England and people knew that anytime the USA would be drug into it.

Harold LaMotte Eustice was so different form Noveline. He was out going, very handsome and having a great personality. Heads turned when he walked into a room. He was stationed in Texas and made many trips to Minden to see his wife who was pregnant. He was really pleased that I was a girl, they were debating what my middle name would be Ann or Jean. He came into the hospital room and said I just put down on her birth certificate that her middle name is Ann.

He was there in Texas when he got the news he was being sent overseas to England as a bombardier, on his third mission the plane was shot down and he was captured by the Germans and was in a concentration camp for nine months.

Because the Army/Air Corps did not know if he was alive or not they sent all of his personal effects. What a blow to find he had been living with a WAC as man and wife.

When the war ended and he was released he went home to Beardstown, IL to see his Daddy called, Pop. Daddy didn't want to return to his wife and Pop said you have an obligation to your wife and daughter, and sent him to Minden.

He and my uncle Emmet bought a fleet of dump trucks, Mama financed the venture. Sadly it went belly up and Mama lost all of her money. He enrolled into Tech University and because of Mother being a nurse, Tech made her the nurse of the men's dormitory and they made them a nice apartment next to the infirmary and she was on call twenty four-seven.

At Christmas I wanted to get up to see what Santa had brought me but Daddy and my uncle wouldn't let me up, seems they were enjoying the eclectic train too much !

He was in his third year at Tech, I had come over on the bus to see them and he said he wanted to gas up the car and get a case of cokes. My Mother and I looked out the window waiting for his return. This is something I'd do for the rest of my life - looking for someone to return to me.

Thirty days later my Mother got divorce papers. She told me that the reason he left us was because I was a girl. He remarried quickly and had a son which validated the fact that he wanted a boy and not me. That one remark would forever change how I looked at myself. This added to the insecurities that would forever change me.

When I was nine he called and asked if he could come to Shreveport and take me out for the day? My Mother said yes he could. He came and he was everything I thought a Daddy should be. We went to a fancy hotel where he had a room and first we went to the restaurant and had breakfast. Then he bought the Sunday paper and read it, then in the afternoon he took me to a movie at the Strand Theater. I don't remember the movie, but I could take you to where we sat, during the movie he reached over and took my hand and held it. I fell in love with my Daddy that day!

The things that people did in my life made for a insecure child/adult. My Mother was the sum total of her fears. In other words she was an insecure, neurotic, slightly mad woman. What was so surprising was she was an excellent Registered Nurse. My uncle told me that she had fallen on concrete when she was twelve and was knocked out for a time.

His observation was after the fall and as she grew up, her actions many time was that of a twelve year old, emotionally she was twelve. This would explain her actions. I didn't know this until I was grown. I wonder had I known could I have understood her better

We got a surprise call from my Daddy he and his family had returned from Japan. He wanted me to come and stay for two weeks and meet his family. I was allowed to go and my aunt Mary Alice and Mama drove me to meet Daddy in Texas, and he drove me the rest of the way to meet his wife and sons.

When I first met his wife, the first thing I asked her was she Martel Dunn? (Martel Dunn was the WAC that Daddy had been living with as husband and wife.)There were three brothers, John, Timmy and Eddie, now it was Eddie that got my full attention, he was six weeks old and his bassinette was I the living room and I was sleeping on the couch. (It never dawned on me that she put me on the couch and her sons had beds) In the night he began to cry so I got up with him and put his bottle on to warm and I changed him.

When Jackie came into the living room there I sat with that precious baby rocking him and giving him his bottle. I told her to go back to bed I would take care of Eddie. So, he became my baby for those two weeks and then plans were made for us to move to California

What my Daddy said to my Mother about her moving to California is sheer speculation. I think he told her he would leave Jackie for her since he had left her for Jackie. How foolish my Mother was to believe that he would be still in love with her and would leave his wife and family for her!

Daddy and family drove to Minden to pick me up at my Mama's house. (My Aunt Mary Alice was the sweetest, kindest woman in the world, and to my knowledge the only time she was ever rude to anyone.) But it was done in such a way that if you didn't know her you wouldn't have known, for above all she was a lady she had listened to me cry as a child asking why wasn't I enough for him. Because of all of that she did blame Jackie for my Daddy leaving me and my Mother.

The trip began with us headed to Beardstown, IL where my Daddy and Jackie had grown up, also where my granddad Pop Eustice lived there. All of Jackie's sisters lived there. Their names are Mary, Eleanor and Sally. They treated me like I was part of their family as did Jackie. She was very kind to me when I misbehaved she would correct me as she did the boys. During this time I began to love her.

I had a cousin named Jon, he and I went on a paddle boat down the river. Eleanor was in charge of us and her being deaf made it hard to communicate with her.

Of course I was ornery, Jon was too, but it was because of me. We were twelve (back when children who were twelve were ignorant of worldly things such as sex).

When we got home from the boat we went and laid down to take a nap. He and I were in the same bed. Eleanor about had a fit! We couldn't figure out why? We were cousins! Later on we found out that she thought we were sexually attracted to each other!! Oh! My! Evil minds. That one incident took some of the closeness that we had away. Yet as long as I came back with the family Jon I was good friends.

On the trip to California, it was very long and very tiresome, Daddy drove like he flew airplanes, fast as we were going around a mountain and Jackie was on her knees in the front seat taking care of Eddie when Daddy had to slam on his brakes, had he not reached out and put his arm around her she would have gone through the windshield.

After that scare I took care of Eddie, I was in the back seat next to him anyway and taking care of Eddie again was wonderful. He knew who I was and he loved me as much as I loved him. I spoiled him rotten, he would see me and try to talk to me, it was precious.

Now this was love! Finally, we arrived at Mather Air Force Base just outside of Sacramento. The Air Force had base housing for us, and all of the furniture came, got put away and it was a nice place to live. It had a huge back yard and was a nice place for me to take care of the boys in the yard. We spent a lot of time in that yard.

When it was time for baths I bathed them all, big boys in the tub Eddie in the kitchen sink. He and I shared a room and as he got older and would wake up he wanted my attention and if I didn't wake up he would take the nipple of the bottle and swing it at me sometimes hitting me in the head! Thankfully the bottle would be empty so it didn't hurt much when he hit his target. What could I expect I was his main caregiver and that pleased me greatly.

After some time Mother rented a little basement apartment it was so small and compared to Daddy house it was awful, but all she could afford. (At that time Nurses didn't make that much money)

It was then that the attacks on Jackie began, if I made the mistake of having fun and telling her, I caught it because Jackie broke up our home. We would've been living well had Daddy stayed with us. It was hard on me for I did love Jackie and I loved her loving me. As the attacks increased so did the distance between Jackie and I grew.

We (the family) moved off base into a nicer house, I still shared a room with Eddie, but that was ok for he was my baby. Often Daddy was off flying on the weekends leaving me Jackie and the boys. I hated going when Daddy wasn't there, even though I love the brothers.

Somehow Jackie and I got into an argument about John and I told her I was as good as him, even better because I was the first born! She was very angry with me and called me a bitch. I went to the phone and called my Mother at work, told her what had happened she told me to pack call a cab come by the hospital for the money to pay the cab and get the key to the apartment. While I was for the cab, Jackie tried to make up with. There was not any making up that day!

When Daddy got home he asked where is Samantha? (The year I was twelve that was his pet name for me and I never knew why). What Jackie told him I do not know but he called my Mother and she related to him what she had called me, that I didn't want to come over anymore unless he was home, for not only was I care taker of the boys I also had to clean house. That put more of a strain on our relationship. (I don't think that Daddy was aware that I was a babysitter and a maid)

Though she did try and from time to time we seemed close again. I so regret that my Mother was constantly undermining Jackie, for there seemed to be no hope for us to become friends again. I feel that Jackie did love me but I was like a cactus hard to get close to again.

There we some fun times too. Daddy taught me how to slow dance and it was so much fun. I had already gotten to about five foot six and one half. Jackie was five feet tall and Daddy said it was fun dancing with me because I was tall. He love to pop corn and us watch tv together all of us sitting around. We did have a lot of fun then.

Then Daddy bought a new home in Rancho Cordova not too far from the base. It was a dream house. It had 3 bedrooms, a formal dining room with beautiful furniture and hutch that showed off all of the china dishes they had gotten in Japan. It also had a formal living room and a huge family room, washer and dryer in the double car garage. Only one car Jackie refused to learn how to drive.

I really loved my brothers. It was close to three years when my Mother realized that a future with Daddy was never going to take place. Friends of ours lived in Houma, La and they agreed to let us go with them and Mother would help on the cost of the trip back to Shreveport. I missed my Daddy and the brothers so much for I was their big sister and they loved me as well.

Although I would miss my Daddy and his family I knew that my Mother could never be an officer's wife. Jackie had started out with Daddy when he was a first Lt, and as he climbed the ranks she learned to a good wife socially and to be around other officers including and ones with much higher ranks, ones in charge of his life.

Husband Number One

It was 1957 when I had a first date with a boy, whom we had met at one of my stepfather's cousins. I got to Fair Park High School and he was there and started asking me out. Finally my Mother said we could date, she felt since she had met his Mother it would be ok. His name was JM he was eighteen and a grown man (although he was really short I was almost and inch taller that he was) he wanted to "make out " more than I was comfortable with. It came down to he wanted to have sex.

Now I was a good Southern Baptist girl and I knew that pre-marital sex was a no-no. If you did have sex I thought my belly button would unscrew and my legs would fall off. Giggle! There was no argument that he could give me that would make me have sex with him.

Life with my Mother was very hard she was verbally and physically abusive to me and I thought that if we got married I would escape her once and for all. I told my Mother that JM and I wanted to get married of course she said no. I blurted out I was pregnant, I always wondered why she didn't take me to the doctor to confirm if I was pregnant, but she didn't and before you know it my Aunt Alice was in on it and was helping us to get the show on the road.

We went to Sears to find a dress (only charge card Mother had) and we looked and looked and I found a cute black one. Neither Mother nor I realized how inappropriate choosing a black dress was. Although it did seem to really mean this farce had no hope at all, so perhaps choosing the black dress was the right thing after all. This was a mistake that no one else in our family would make.

We went to Marshall, Texas to get married, he was a justice of the Peace and he said more than once he thought he knew JM and had seen him before. JM was very good at lying and making people believe him. But the fact of the matter JM had been at this same place getting married in May 1957!

I sure would like to say we lived happily ever after, but children really have no chance, I wish someone would hear what I am saying and would never do this foolish thing. When he told his parents they were really unhappy. REALLY UNHAPPY! I didn't understand their not liking me. They insisted that JM lived at his house and I with my Mother. We agreed for a while, and then he more or less moved me in. It was different than anyplace I had ever seen. There were four rooms, two bedrooms. Thankfully for me I got to sleep with his sister Nancy, she was wonderful actually more than wonderful. I realized I had moved into white trash. His father was a painter, his mother worked at a very smart dress shop, when she went out of the house to go to work you would never know where she lived or the conditions. As soon as they were both there the yelling began, they seemed to hate each other. They had a total of six kids and JM was their pet, no matter what kind of trouble he got into they got him out!

He wouldn't work so I called my Daddy and asked him if we could come to live there until he got a job and we found a place to live. He said we could, he had told my Mother in no way let me get married! We took the bus from Shreveport to Sacramento, it was a long trip and I was pregnant not very far along but enough to be miserable. Daddy picked us up at the bus station. One look at JM and I knew he didn't like him he knew he was a punk! He did show his dislike for him, but it rolled off of JM's back like a duck off water.

Daddy at that time was Club Officer at the Officers Club, so he got JM a job as a janitor, two reasons so he could keep up with him and try to protect me. Daddy finally found us a room with a small kitchen, it was in a trailer park and to go to the bathroom, shower had to go about five hundred feet. We had no entertainment and there was a lady with 3 children and when she opened her curtains that meant I could come over. I know she felt sorry for me knowing my husband's ways and being with child at fifteen. She saved my sanity.

I craved cheese toast, fries and eggs as soon as they hit bottom off I went to throw up, he always seemed so much further and so glad that I always made it. One day I said something that ticked off JM and he slapped me. I was telling Daddy how sick I was feeling and mentioned that JM had slapped me. One night about ten thirty there was a knock on the door. JM got up he was in his underwear and t-shirt and there stood my Daddy. He yanked up JM by the t-shirt and put him into a corner then put his knee in the lowest area of his underwear, told him I never hit her and you had better NEVER hit her again.

He was a lousy worker but he had a line for the lady's and soon he was dating a young First LT. Of course when Daddy found out he was livid. One day JM didn't come home called Daddy at the Club and he said he wasn't at work, but had gotten paid. Seems he decided to leave and go back to Shreveport. Because of this I moved back in with the family. Once again I became sole caretaker of the boys and house cleaner, while Jackie talked on the phone most of the day drinking king sized cokes, and making fun of the child bride. She was pretty open with her disgust for me, not when Daddy was around though.

I always found this funny. Daddy made her iron their sheets and pillow cases, along with his undershirt and shorts! So when she wasn't on the phone laughing at me, she did do the ironing. One day I was going somewhere with Daddy and I was in the back seat and I found a high heel. I hid it, because I had been over to a Colonel's wife visiting and I saw all of her shoes, so I knew right away whose shoe it was. I went over to visit and gave her back her shoe. Why didn't I tell Jackie? Well, the child bride who was so darned funny didn't think she deserved to know whom my Daddy was seeing.

Jackie demanded that I vacuum the whole house everyday including the formal dining room that was never used. It was excessive and frankly she was being mean to me. One morning I woke up with the worst morning sickness, and her she was telling me to vacuum and I told her I was just too sick to do anything. An argument began and I finally I told her if she didn't leave me alone I would kick her butt. She ran as fast as she could to call Daddy, came back into the living room and said your Dad wants to talk to you, then she ran back to the bedroom so she could hear what was said. I told Daddy how I cleaned the house vacuumed all of the house when it wasn't needed and that I was so sick and just couldn't work for her right then and I said I had told her if she didn't leave me alone I would kick her butt ! She was on the other line and Daddy knew it and he said Jackie leave her alone, she is sick and not your maid, watch out for she just might kick your butt!!

When Christmas time came she went all out for the boys, two to three hundred on each boy and she gave me a carton of cigarettes and at the base they were about three dollars. But I loved my brothers so much that I delighted in their presents.

Daddy was to go to some bases in southern California and he took me with him, we had a blast! When we went to Los Angles we went to the Macomb night club. Someone touched my elbow and it was Tennessee Ernie Ford, Daddy leaned over and said don't you dare! After we were seated the waiter came over for our drink order I said I would have a Tom Collins and he said she will have a coke. There were lots of movie stars there and we also saw Walter Winchell. It was great. Then Daddy put me on a bus to Shreveport and was once again home bound.

When JM realized I was back in town he insisted that I move back in with the family. I did so and then and there Nancy and I cemented a relationship that has lasted all of this time I love her more today than back then. I had lots of clothes and I told Nancy to wear all she wanted, when we went to California I had left some clothes, she was so glad because she didn't have many clothes and I loved seeing her looking so pretty in my clothes.

When summer came we were left alone with the youngest Rea and we ate and had fun all day long. When it was about time for the family to come home we jumped up and got it clean in short order. We had so much fun together. One day I was making the bed and there was a knock at the door it was a young woman and she wanted to see JM so I went out to the back to the tire shop (they re-grooved tires for re-sell) and told him there was a woman at the door named Dottie and she wanted to see JM. They locked me in that tire shed. It was so hot and summer time too. Later on I found out that was his other wife.

I decided to go to the charity hospital, although Mother said she would pay for me to go to a good doctor but I said this is my fault so I won't let you pay for my mistake. One day the black people came for treatment and to visit the next day was for the whites. It was awful; they treated you like cattle, and were very demeaning. I was taking the trolley home and as we turned a corner there was JM with his arm around another girl pulled really close to him. My heart broke when I saw that, after being at the hospital and treated so badly then to see him. My little fifteen year old heart couldn't take it. I got off the trolley prepared to transfer so I could go to the house. There was a Woolworth's there and I stood just inside by the door and when JM and girl came past I stepped out and asked him did he want to introduce his wife? The girl took off running and that was the day that I learned to hate JM.

In August it was so hot, my due date was July 13, but was still big pregnant. One night I woke up with horrible pains scared Nancy badly, she went and got her mother, she proceeded to make herself a cup of coffee, smoke and fix her face. Finally she called a cab and the driver went over the railroad tracks really slow. She said drive fast and get her there, when we got to the hospital he said no charge just get out of my cab! I had called Mother and told her to meet us there and in her uniform hoping she could go into the delivery room with me. They didn't allow her to do that and forty five minutes later I gave birth to a daughter, weighting seven pounds and fourteen ounces. The doctor that delivered her was really young and when she first came out, she came out crying and I leaned up and said what is it? He said what do you want I said it has to be a girl, he said let's get this baby out of here so we can see her sex. Bless God it was a girl. He slapped her on her behind and said remember this; William Kamback Jr. was the first man to lay a hand on your daughter! We had been alone the whole time and the nurse came in and was surprised that I had delivered so quickly. Dr said do you know how old she is and she said no, he said sixteen and she didn't holler like so many of the older ones do.

When I came out of the delivery room I had my knees pulled up and had a leg crossed and as I passed by all, I said did you see what I did? She was born at four am and as it would happen it was colored day so none of my family could come and see me. I managed to walk down to the nurse's station and said get my baby ready I am going home. I called my step dad Harold and said Daddy come and get us. When he walked in the hospital the guards said you can't be here. He said my baby called me to come and get her and her baby and that's what I am going to do, I think they knew they didn't want to cross this man. So he took my baby and me to Mother's apt and when the family found out I was there they insisted that I come there to live.

Her daddy would yell and scream at me and I would just go from room to room (only4) and slamming doors as I went. Nancy marveled at this for she was afraid of him when he was yelling! I lived with a man who beat my Mother, yelling didn't scare me and I think he loved that about me that I wouldn't cow down! I loved that man, I really did!

He came home about dinnertime and asked what was I going to cook for supper, there is no food in this house. He began to pull things out of the ref. and together we began to cook supper. That was the beginning of him coming home every day. He taught me how to cook. It was plain food that stuck to your ribs. We had a crowd to feed! He made a good cook out of me, I still love to cook and if I cook something he taught me I loved remembering him, his son NOT AT ALL do I ever miss!!

When school was out began my fun life in living with them, Nancy and I had this dirty house to clean, no one believed in taking a dish to the sink, pick up dirty clothes, it fell to us to clean it all. At this time I was craving French fried sandwiches with lots of Miracle Whip on them. I got Nancy and Rea hooked on them. Later I found out she ate them all the time not knowing I was just craving!!

We set the clock when we needed to start cleaning the house, and off we would go and we made it fun. We got it clean and the minute they walked in it was dirty again, sigh.
We feed them, cleaned up the table so they could drink coffee, the mom smoked and for her to get ready it took several cups of coffee and lot of smoking

When I could no more stand him, I escaped to my Mothers. He came in one night to our apartment and took my daughter at knife point. I had to go to court to get her back, what a farce. JM had a guy from the base swear he was with him and that my Mother was going to give her a shot (my Mother almost her Nursing License for that lie, thank God she was reputable) and he said on the stand they went out the back door. We only had one door. Finally they got a crooked attorney. (They kept one to get JM out of all of his jams). He fixed it so I had to take my daughter to the mom's day care. I went three months without seeing my daughter. When I saw her she was sitting up, had her shoe off and looked up at me with those big brown eyes, she didn't know me at first but finally she did. I kept up to her plan for a while and then quit and about that time she shut down the day care.

She would continually try to keep my daughter and finally at eleven she had been seeing JM secretly and he convinced her to run away. She got in touch with the step mother and she refused to let her come and live with them. She was keeping him for he was really too lazy to work, although she bought him a garage to fix cars, a long haul truck to drive over the road. None of these things did he work at as he should. There were constantly women and she knew it, he had threatened to kill her, I knew he wouldn't kill her just beat her up but she is still with him. Unbelievable to me, guess I wasn't as dumb as I thought at sixteen!

Husband Number Two

I worked at this bar as a waitress, and there I met a man who looked like Robert Mitchum and was six foot four! The attraction was so strong to each other it wasn't long before we were dating and sleeping together. He had a sister that was eleven years younger and a brother that was eleven years younger than her. She and my daughter shared the same name so mine was called ......baby, to keep them separate when calling them. Before long I was living with them and took care of the little brother. His mother decided that we would get married and I had planned to get away from him because he had slapped me and made me afraid. But the marriage train took on a life of its own. So here I am married again at seventeen and a half. He was a drunk and loved the women and they loved him, he wouldn't come home and stay out drinking and coming home smelling like the woman he had been with. We had a boy when we had been married about a year. The life with him was violent, and he did beat me.

I would leave him, take the kids and go to my Mother's I tended bar and one night he came and took my baby boy, him I didn't see till he was five, nine months old when he left with him. I talked to RJ and asked could I send my boy Christmas presents and he said sure, but I have told him you are dead!

He called me out of the blue and asked would I come to Houston to visit with him. I went and stayed 2 months and finally my Mama told me to get home, but I came home pregnant with our second child. My Mama was so mad at me for getting pregnant. He finally came and got my daughter and we went to live with him. The bar life never stopped and nor did the womanizing. Finally I gave birth to a second son, a big boy.

This womanizing and fighting getting beat up went on for eleven years. All total we probably lived together for five years. Back and forth we went (I was a slow learner). One time after returning to him I got pregnant very quickly and he said it wasn't his baby but it was. I knew that if I gave birth to that child there would never be any peace for he just didn't think it was his. I had gone to church on Sunday morning, and all of this time I was doing things to my body to abort the baby. I woke up Monday morning so sick, running a high fever, and two ladies from the church came to see me. I had kept my daughter home to take care of my little son. They knew I was sick but didn't know the reason for the sickness. They said to call them if I needed them. I went next door to call one of them and my water broke and the lady of the house said get out I don't want that on my new carpet! I went back home and sent my daughter to call one of the ladies and she agreed to take me to the hospital. When I got there I saw the Gynecology Doctor on call. When he asked me what I had done to myself, I said make all of the people leave the room. (I knew they could read the report). I just didn't want to say it out loud in front of them. He did some tests, put me on some heavy antibiotic and sent me to a private room. I knew that I should have the baby soon. A nurse's aide was so precious to me. I asked her what did she think would happen if I were to bear down? I tried that and I began to bleed profusely and began filling up one bed pan after another, she begged me not to say that we had talked about it I assured her I wouldn't tell. After many of these I was without a bed pan and a stinging was at the door of the womb. I took my mirror out of my purse and looked. There was the baby encased in the sac and I could see the baby plainly it was well formed. I hit the speaker and said someone should get her quickly I have done something. They looked and went after a container, when RJ finally did show up to see me, the Doctor asked him does she have any family? She just might not make it, RJ did call my Mother and the Doctor did a DNC and I was fine. I went home and RJ cared not one bit that I almost died, or lost the baby. It seemed every commercial was about babies, I went into a deep depression but he never even noticed. He had been dating a girl before I came back to him this time, she ended up carrying the baby ten months they forced a delivery and she delivered a dead baby boy. My husband went on a three day drunk. I almost died and he didn't care. I left him he called me at my Mothers house and ask me to come home. I told I knew about the dead baby and I would never live with him again.

Husband Number Three

I had moved with the boys to Kansas City, Kansas and I worked for a FM radio station that had people selling ads for the radio. I went out and collected the money and took down what they wanted to say about their business. I was dating two men, one knew about the other, they both worked for the same company.

Pretty soon I had this man began to making passes at me, I explained I had too much on my plate to add a third. DH was very persistent and often we played pool together. One night there was some people at a booth and he came over for us to play pool. It seemed on the ladies was his ex-wife and after our pool game she said she is the one? He wouldn't respond. The company was moving to Texas to work FM stations there and I didn't go.

I went to work tending bar, finally started dating him and he moved us in together. He was wonderful and became my best friend. We were really in love with each other, he would stop at the bar, but he didn't cheat. We were so happy and one afternoon there was a knock at the door, there stood my son with an older man. He had gone over to play ball with his friend and the dad came out and my son pitched the ball to the dad and he hit the ball the ball hit my son in the nose. His face was swollen and his nose was huge we took him to the ER but the doctors said he had to have surgery and they didn't have anyone capable to do that on staff, so they gave him pain pills and sent him home. He slept on the couch and kept an ice bag on him the next day we had the referral to the Nose Specialist and he said he would have to have some delicate surgery. I wish I could say that while he was in surgery. I stayed there and waited. But we went drinking calling the hospital and when he was in the hospital I went every day for the nine days he was there. I was a bad mother, and worse I knew it but couldn't handle life without the drinking.

We were both morning people, I would bring him a cup of coffee and go and bring the pot and we would talk for as long as we could before he went to work. He taught me how to cure a hangover. Go have another drink and there is a thin line between getting well and getting drunk again. I have never met anyone who could hold his booze so well.

On football Sundays we would fix tv trays with all sorts of goodies and I would cook a big Sunday Dinner. The boys enjoyed those times. We also loved the drive in movies; I would pop corn, fix hot dogs, but them back in the bun with the dressing on them and put them back in the bun bag to keep them warm. We also had pop in our cooler and of course beer. Usually the first movie would be more family minded then the next two were geared to adults, not x of course but would later be rated as R.

We had started going to an Assembly of God Church pretty regularly and I loved it and so did the boys. One Sunday morning C. M. Ward was there Preaching and he called us out and said that God had a call on our life. At that time it didn't make much of a difference in out lives but we were Church active.

I got pregnant and had a blue eyed boy and he was a charmer from day one. DH and I were having trouble because I became obsessed with him; I told him that I loved him more than God. Although I wasn't serving God we did go to church and pray before meals, and sometimes read the Word. God is a jealous God and I had made promises to Him and He keeps up with them.

DH was having an affair with one then another; I got pregnant again but didn't really think I was. I was drinking more, had worse hangovers and threw up constantly and worked tending bar. I went to the Dr because I had a really bad upper chest and sinus infection. I ask the Dr to check with the stethoscope and he said I can hear fetal heart beats what do you think? I asked him how far along I was and he said about five months. Now abortions were legal in Kansas, I got home drunk and looked up an abortion clinic. I called and when I did and the phone picked up a new born baby cried!! About that time DH came in I told him to call the number and he said it gave the times of the business hours. I told him about the baby crying and I said I am going to have this baby maybe it will be my girl. He said it's your body do as you please.

Well Bless God I had the most beautiful little girl, her birth weight was small but she was fine. (At that time there were no precautions about drinking and having fetal alcohol syndrome). She did get sick and had the whooping cough; she got sick after the first shot so we couldn't complete them. She weighted fourteen pounds and was four months old. The Dr admitted her, when the nurse was helping to undress her she gasped and asked what I had on her toenails, hot pink fingernail polish! They thought she was a new born for she weight seven pounds! She was in the hospital about a week and she was sent home, my Dr had taken a young Dr and he had given me and children to him. I got home with her and she would cough turn blue and pass out. I called my Dr and said I don't mind his building up his practice but I won't let him kill my baby. He had me go back and she was readmitted, when the Dr took her out from under the oxygen hood he was holding her and she began to cough and turn blue and pass out. As he held her he kept saying "oh baby I didn't realize how sick you were, I am so sorry, (he carried on like that for a while) she ended up staying for twenty one days. And finally she got to come home and was ok then. It was so scary because I thought she would die. Thank you God for healing my precious baby girl!

The beatings were pretty regular now, and though I still loved him with all my heart, we couldn't keep from fussing. I was so depressed at the thought of losing him but I knew it was just a matter of time. But, he couldn't stay away from me nor I from him.

I was working and the woman he was seeing was smaller than I was but I had had two babies back to back they were eleven months and fifteen days apart. So, I began if I drank I couldn't eat, if I ate I couldn't drink. I lost fifty pounds pretty quickly, thought there I had the better figure! Then I began to have constant pains in my lower back no matter how drunk I got I couldn't drink enough to stop the pain. I went to the Dr and asked for a pap smear, I had a feeling I had cancer (I truly believe that God made me aware so I wouldn't die).

The Dr's office called and said I had to come in right then, it was on a Friday afternoon. I ran out of the bar and the Dr said the pap smear looked bad that I had to go to the hospital on Sunday pm to be admitted and have further tests done. I had to have a piece of my uterus removed and tested. The results were I had cervical cancer and it was spread to all of my female organs. I had surgery three days later, DH had found someone who would board the little ones, he had agreed to stay home with my boys. He came in one morning and I knew he had stayed at his girlfriend's house. I got so upset that the Nurses said I had to get control of myself, but I threw him out and told him to stay with his whore. I was in the hospital for twelve days and I didn't have a way home so I called DH and he came and got me. (Before I went into surgery I was pretty loopy and I called his girl friend whom I knew well and asked her didn't she want to wish me bad luck?) Before the sedation I went down to the Chapel and asked God not to let me die, to let me raise my children, I promised all sorts of things, but after the surgery I didn't keep my promise. Four months later I had to have my gall bladder removed. DH put the little ones back where they had stayed when I had the first surgery.

DH pretty much left me that time for good although he kept seeing me, and would get my babies all upset when he left them. He finally found a woman who didn't drink and was pretty passive about what he did. My only problem with her was she didn't like my daughter because she looked like me, one time she wanted DH to whip my daughter because she didn't finish a sandwich. I told DH if she ever did that again I would take action, it never happened again and of course he catered to her children. She was good to my son because he went up there to live with them.

Husband Number Four

A friend called me and wanted me to come to Columbia Mo and meet a man that she had met. I went we were not impressed with each other because he was cocky and sure of himself as I was. I loved spending time with her and I met her friend and the longer I knew him the better I liked DC.

After I went back to KC, he called and wanted me and my children to move there and live with him. He really showed me a good side of himself, and I knew I would never get DH back so I thought what did it matter? He called every night and kept saying he would find us a place to live, finally he said for me to come and find us a place. I found a really nice three bedroom mobile home to live in .And I thought if I didn't like him I would leave him I knew I could go to work at any bar I wanted to, I was a really good bartender !

He hadn't found a job and he went to see his folks in his home town about a hundred miles from Columbia. I stayed at home, if fact one of his best friends and his girl friend were going to KC so I found a sitter and I went with them. Saw DH out drinking and he was friendly but not friendly enough for my taste. We got back to Columbia late and I get a call from DC wanting me to drive and get him he had gotten really sick and wanted to see a Dr at Columbia.

So hung over away I went I found the farm easily by the directions given. I don't think I made a good impression because I had left over booze on my breath, and my long hair didn't help first impressions. I like his parents, thought they were nice people, didn't meet his brother then, his only sibling.

When we got back to Columbia a woman that lived next door saw how bloated he was and her husband had the same problem and she recommended a Heart Dr. His name was Dr Polite and it was just a miracle that the Dr we were supposed to see was in a car wreck and we saw his partner, who had a really great reputation. DC had been born a blue baby so his health was always precarious, he had open heart surgery in Chicago when he was seven, The Dr was only able to keep him on the table long enough to open a valve that was closed but told his parents he had holes in his heart that would have to be fixed someday.

Dr Polite told DC if he ever lied to him about anything he would dismiss him. So DC told him of a drug problem that he had, shooting up heroin he was able to kick it cold turkey because he was in jail , the lady jailer saw something in him. After his two roommates beat him up badly she had him put into a separated cell, would bring him cigarettes and food. When it was time for him to get out she took him to her home helped him find a place to live after he found a job. He still smoked weed, and drank lots and over ate. Dr Polite put him in the hospital and put him on an iv drip to take off the excess water. By morning he had lost forty pounds. He kept loosing till he was back to normal weight and when he was released it was with a lot of medicine.

The next time we went to the farm I took my kids with me, they were almost two and three. Neither one of the boys had any children. My daughter used cloth diapers so I had to really work at keeping her clean, my son loved his new papaw. He would go out with papaw and DC and sometimes the brother would be there. As soon as they got back they would be hot and sweaty so I would put them both in a tub and get them smelling good again. The brother did ask how it was that the kids never smelled bad. His mom said Barbara keeps them really clean, he said he had never been around kids that were always so good smelling. (I kept them clean at home too, this wasn't a show off).

One time the brother brought his girlfriend Sherri with him, I didn't realize how much his mom disliked her but if looks of hatred worked, she'd be dead! All of us got a long and one day the dam broke and I say them all in action, the way the dad, the boys treated the mother was shameless, from the time she hit the floor was total verbal abuse, it was awful, she was a Christian and tried to live her life as one.

The dad was crippled and loved that he had horses and cattle, and why not? The mom took care of everything and had to take care of the animals before she went and taught school, and when she got home not only did she have to prepare the meal she had to tend to the animals She told me one time she married because she felt so sorry for him. Oh! This is never a reason to marry, if they guilt trip you before marriage just wait it hasn't even started yet. He would plow and she would plant and take care of the garden, including canning everything, she was one super woman. Often I heard that she stayed at school late, I understood there was quiet there, no verbal abuse. He made fun of everyone but himself and of course his precious sons.

The brother was short and overbearing to DC, he acted so superior (as often happens with short man syndrome). He acted like he loved the kids, but I have come to believe he only loves the person he sees in the mirror. He wanted to play sports in high school and the dad wouldn't let him, and I think that was just many chips on his shoulders. It was funny DC adored him, bragged how popular he had been in high school, dated cheer leaders. Sheri made a big deal over the kids at Christmas time, now looking back they were both good actors. In fact one day Sheri and I was in mom's bedroom and she began to talk ugly about mom. I said don't say that, she is wonderful! She looked at me like I had lost my mind and said you really do love her don't you? I said yes, she is the closest thing to a mother I ever had.

I had gone out drinking one night and had vomited and passed out in the car, woke up it was morning. Went home and my daughter had soiled herself and he wouldn't change her. We had talked of marriage but I was trying to figure a way to escape him for now I was verbally abused constantly. I was so sick, hung over he said lets get married, I said ok just so he would go to work. He came home with a marriage license once again I am on a runaway train to marriage. Oh there was just no getting out of it.

Strange in all of my marriages I had never been married before a Preacher, always a Justice of the Peace. When we went to the farm and told mom that we had gotten married she wasn't really happy about it, however she loved my daughter so very much and I think she made herself happy because she would really be her granddaughter. It was funny that when DC's brother married Sheri made her think my marriage was a good thing. Giggle. She had wanted her son to remarry his first wife. Mom treated Sheri way better than she deserved.

Before we moved to his home town, we were drunk as skunks and went to visit an old friend of his. Apparently there was a woman there. I was too drunk to remember meeting her. After we left their house, the wife said they are really good Christians. Of course, Martha didn't share her opinion of me as a Christian.

After we moved to his home town and there was a fun night for the children, bike races all sorts of fun things for them. The woman came up to me and said you are DC's wife? Yes I am, she introduced herself to me, and I said we have something in common. She sort of put her nose up in the air and said really? Yes I said, Jesus! That was the beginning of a wonderful friendship that I will always value!

DC was in and out of the hospital every few months, finally Dr Polite put a pace maker in his heart. That worked for some time and he was able to go back to hanging sheet rock sooner than anyone expected. He did continue to smoke, and that sure wasn't good for his heart. He was supposed to manage his liquid intake, but he just couldn't do that. Dr Polite wanted him to have a heart transplant but his refusal to obey the Dr's orders. His nurse Marion Sherman got to one side one of the times he was in the hospital and she told me there was no way he could have a heart, since he wouldn't do as the Dr demanded she, said there is no use wasting a good heart on someone who would just abuse it. I never told DC or his parents.

He had open heart surgery and Dr Polite put Dacron patches on the holes in his heart. I decided to stay and a friend of mine offered me a car and a spare bedroom. That night after the surgery I was sleeping on the couch in the waiting room and the nurse came and got me and said they were going to have to reopen him, the heart wasn't used to having that much blood flow and the veins burst and he was bleeding to death. I asked to see him, I had noticed before the outtake hose had been trickling fluid. When I went in to see him it was like a flood of blood in the outtake hose.

When his parents came for a visit and the brothers first wife, I stressed to them please when you go in there don't act like he is dying. He is so much improved now, they went in and his mom and ex sister in law went on something terrible. When we went outside I asked them how could you do that to him? Now he thinks he is dying because of how you reacted in there. His dad went in and tried to make it better. When they went home I went in and told him, look you are sitting up, eating ice cream don't you know you are on the mend? I finally got him calmed down, his brother didn't come to see him anytime he was in the hospital, too busy to see his brother.

The health insurance we had paid very little on the bill. After insurance paid we owed them $ 8,000.00. They sent us a letter saying they would reduce it to $ 3,000.00 if we paid it in full. I went to see them and said we don't have the money. The next offer was $ 1800.00 again I explained we didn't have the money. I paid ten dollars on it for years, at Christmas 1984 I had finally paid off the balance and had the check that said paid in full. I framed it and gave it to him as one of his Christmas presents. He wept.

His pacemaker quit making seed and he went into congestive heart failure, had to be taken to the hospital in an ambulance, what we found out later they almost lost him and the ambulance had to stop to take care of him. The next day he went into surgery to have the pace maker moved to another location in his chest, He was in the hospital for forty one days that time. He would go into congestive heart failure often.

He was really sick right after Christmas and was admitted to the hospital. I got a call from Marion Sherman, the nurse and said I needed to come to the hospital they were losing him. It was a blizzard and I told her I couldn't come that night but would be there in the morning when I could see the two lane highway before getting on the interstate. When I got there I waited for Dr Polite, I ask him if you were me should I get my children up here to see their daddy? He said yes. I went to the pay phone and called my mother in law and asked her to bring the children and if she couldn't I would come home and get them, she realized how bad it was and said no, she would dress the children and bring them up to see him as they wanted to see him as well. The brother called and asked should he come told him what the Dr had said but told him he had to make the choice. That night I couldn't sleep so my friend PE made me a thermos of coffee. I was sitting on the floor drinking coffee. I guess the smell of the coffee woke him up. He asked what was I doing there and I said I felt I should be there with him. We began to talk; he said it hasn't all been bad has it? No I said we have had some wonderful times, the four of us. He looked at me and asked me was he dying and I said yes. His next remark fooled me. He said I don't want to miss my babies growing up. I told him God has pulled you through many times and if its His Will He will pull you through again. He wasn't going to miss his parents, the brother he adored, his wife, but his babies!

Later that night he went into a cardiac coma, they put him in a recliner that was for heart patients. They moved him to a room across from the Nurses station. I went to my friends and took a shower, went back to the hospital and was reading the paper and I noticed the date it was January 7, I said that is the number of God. I heard in my spirit that He would take him around one a clock, I ask the Lord to let me know so I could hold his hand as he crossed over, and would he send his grandparents and my aunt Mary Alice, he loved her so much. His parents, brother and his wife were there. (The brother couldn't talk to him since he was in a coma). I was walking around the room drinking coffee and I felt the Spirit telling me to go and hold DC's hand.

I watched when he took his last breath, the nurse was there and I said he is gone. She said not he's not I said yes he's gone. I went out to the Nurses station and all of the nurses were crying for he had been in and out of the hospital for nine and a half years. When he couldn't sleep he would go and sit and visit with the nurses at the station. He was well loved by all of the hospital staff.

It was decided that Sherri would ride home with me, I picked up my clothes at my friends and off we went to drive back to his home town. I know one of the things I said was if I wear my black skirt and black corduroy jacket I'll be a black widow. Whatever else I said I don't remember I know I had been under a lot of strain, not sleeping and going through the death of my husband. What ever I said or didn't say I'm sure Sheri misconstrued what I said. From then on there was a gap between mom and I. One of the hardest things I have ever had to do was forgive Sheri for taking mom away from me. As far as it making mom happier with her, it didn't make a difference she still didn't like Sheri!

As time went on it was harder to live in close proximity to his parents. His dad would use his key and just walk in. I had to put a chain on the door to keep him from walking in on me. Mom was always calling and saying that my son should be mowing the yard or there was always something we were doing wrong.

I decided to move back to LA, my biggest mistake was not asking my kids how they felt about leaving all of their friends and their grandparents. I am so sorry I didn't, but I was just getting worn out from all of the pressure.

Booze, Bars & People Like Me

I worked in bars because that is the only job you can have and work drunk. I was addicted to alcohol by the time I was twenty lead was a life of believing that I was having a good time parting. Men began to pay attention and that fed the insecurity that I had always. The cost was the use of my body, but I thought they really cared about me and I was sure I cared about them. As time went on the indiscreet sex was more frequent and soon it became a way of life. (The worst part of this is when I took a dive into the bottle I took my kids with me and they were in a living hell).

I danced at one bar behind the bar on an elevated platform. The dance of choice was the twist. I was pretty good at it and had a great time, the men really paid attention to me. That fed my ego too. One night there was a girl who was pretty drunk and began throwing pennies at me, when they hit they hurt. Finally I had enough I leaned over and said to her they are paying me to show my butt, who's paying you? Well that got a huge laugh and she left embarrassed. When I lived in IL I worked at a place where we wore fringed bikinis, black fish net hose and really high heels! My daughter was in the first grade and according to a man whose daughter was in the same class, told her class room that I wore a bikini and worked at Stooky Inn. He showed up to find out it was true.

Those were the only jobs I had where I did pretty wild things. I loved to dance and did a lot. I was real funny and more than once the customers would say we'll pay you not to play the juke box and let her rip. I liked being funny some times it was on me sometimes on others, I could remember jokes really well so that played a part in me being a good bar tender.

The interesting thing about being in bars is you get to watch people. I was some times surprised when two couples came in wife's best friend's husband's best friends and one the other husband and wife had it going on and the other set didn't have a clue.

Sex was being done a lot, free love ect. It was amusing to see how people hooked up. I did love to watch all the goings on. It was strange how couples split up because of falling in love, rather lust! One thing I learned quickly and that was men liked long legs and long black hair. I dressed to show my legs at an advantage, I didn't have a great figure but I was normal sized and clothes fit me pretty well because of my height.

When hot pants came out, that was a perfect way to show case my legs, I loved all of the attention that I got. About that time there were two things going on in my world, streaking and partner swapping I never thought that swapping partners was a good idea what was mine I wanted to keep as mine.

It never occurred to me to steak, seems I would come in after they had struck!! I continued tending bar, having indiscreet sex. I figured out why the bars were always dark. Have you ever considered it? It is because satan it the prince of darkness, when people are in the dark they think that they are not as noticeable. Which of course is another deception of his, knowing he is deceptive, has spirits that visit you and causes to lose your inhibitions. Have you ever wondered why a man with a good looking wife would cheat on her with a woman that should bark? Or a woman doing the same, the answer is this. Spirits are chicken they go in twos or threes. For sure Spirits (any form of booze lying and lust). These don't just go away; they have to be prayed off of you.

My experiences that transpired, I have not told you the full of it all, simply because I don't want satan to get any more glory than he got when I was doing all of the things that I did I am not proud of this at all but felt you the Reader had to see the depths of despair that I felt. When I found all of these things out, I realized I had been duped by the master of deception.

Something that is strange that in all of the times of indiscreet sex, I never had any sexual disease. However, when I was married one of my husbands gave me one!

As I lay there in that hospital room I knew I had really blown it, there was no place for me to go, I couldn't return to Louisiana I had been home so many times with failed marriages and relationship's that I just couldn't make myself go home again. As I stewed about what to do, the nurses would come in open the curtains and leave the door open. They'd leave I'd get up close the door and the curtains. I wanted the room as dark as I could get it.

As I lay there the one person I didn't want to see was DC in came in like a storm so very angry that I was in the hospital. Of course he was always angry about something and if he didn't get his way, well he knew how to make our lives miserable!! He demanded that I leave the hospital right then! To his great surprise I refused, he stomped out. I am thinking good riddance!

All of the things I had remembered made me know that I wasn't really worthwhile. I was a looser, big time. Although some the things I had been through had not all been my fault, what happened to me as a child, I was just drug along into that.

One day as I lay there in a fetal position, I heard the Audible Voice of God. To me He said "I have allowed you to knock on the gates of hell, and you need to get off the fence and choose me or the booze "I said I choose you", but in the back of my mind I saw myself having a glass of wine. Then, He said not another drop of anything alcoholic and I said I can't do this alone. Then He said when you get out of the hospital I want you to go and cut your hair. Not my hair!! Yes I am going to change you inside and out!

When I got out of the hospital I went and got my hair cut about my shoulders. When I went back to Church the ladies asked me how old I was and I said thirty-six, and they said they thought that I was between forty and fifty. Now I really didn't understand what had happened in the hospital, and I was cautious not to speak of it. So I told them I had been rode hard and put up wet.

About two weeks later when I was talking to Joanne she asked how the drinking was going and I held the phone and realized that I had no desire for a drink! She started whooping and hollering. She told me from the first time we had met she knew the problem that I had with alcohol!

(Remember the ring? Well Joanne said she had put the ring in my purse. It wasn't there! I went out to look next to the steps and the ground was bare of any grass, we all had looked. I knew cooper would be furious, I went and bought a cheap replacement ring. I promised God, "If you will help get my ring back I promise I will wear it all the time". One evening in my mind I heard the phone ring and it was Joanne. She said she found the ring! The next moment I got the call. When I asked where did she find it she said in the dirt! I truly believe that God had that ring! Once I made the promise I would always wear it, He put it back on the bare ground! What an awesome God I serve).

I had been baptized enough time because I kept answering the call for Salvation, but it just never took.

The Lord explained it to me using Matthew 13:3-8

3 And He spake many things unto them in parables, saying, Behold , a sower went forth to sow:

4 And when he sowed, some seeds fell by the way side, and the fowls came and devoured them up :

5 Some fell upon the stony palces, where they had not much earth:and forthwith they sprung up, because they had no deepness of earth:

6 And when the sun was up, they were scorched; and because they had no root, they withered away.

7 And some fell among thorns; and the thorns sprung up, and chocked them:

8 But other fell into good ground, and brought forth fruit, some an hundredfold, some sixty fold, some thirty fold.

All of the time that I had been drawn to the Holy Spirit it was not good soil. After the talk with God I hungered for the Word as I had booze, it was so good. I loved reading it and would sit on the floor of our mobile home and read and read the Word as my two youngest played at my feet. The television wasn't on, so I could pay attention to them and to the Word as it took deep root in my heart.

I felt I should follow the Lord in baptism, our Church didn't have a baptismal so we borrowed one from another Church, DC wouldn't come and I know satan thought he would dampen me getting baptized,

When my Pastor took me under and then up again I knew that I would never be the same again. I was so glad my friends and children were there to witness this wonderful event. I knew I would never be the same! I found the Peace I had been looking for all of my life. For when people asked me what I wanted when I was drinking, birthday or Christmas gift I would always say, "Peace of Mind".

The Baptism was the fullness I needed for my Salvation. I wish I could say I lived happily ever after. There are always many problems, but I know that God is always there, and nothing can take away my Peace of mind.

Conclusion

What a Mighty God I serve. He can and wants to change you, take away your addictions, but you must

be ready to hand them over to Him and leave the problem in His Mighty Hands and change will come. Some it takes longer than others. Tell me are you happy in your addictions?

There are many programs in help with this; however The Great God Almighty that created you and knew you before you were in your Mother's womb, He knows all about you. I am not knocking these programs, but include God Our Father, or in the Hebrew it means Abba (Daddy)

Writing this book has been painful in some spots to relive the past, and because of my honesty I may hurt my children, for this I am so sorry. The Book, the Title, Chapter Titles have all been given to me by the Precious Holy Spirit and under his direction that it has been written.

My Prayer for you the reader is that you will understand what this is about, written in love and May He touch you in a very Special Way.

Love Barbara

www.ingramcontent.com/pod-product-compliance
Lightning Source LLC
Chambersburg PA
CBHW071428040426
42445CB00012BA/1288